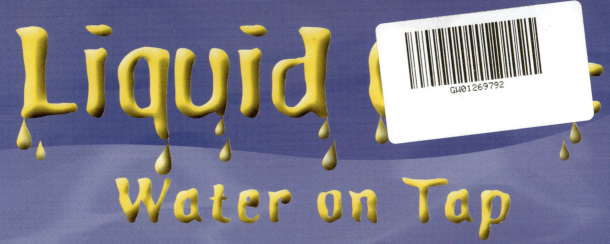

Water on Tap

written by Jillian Powell
illustrated by Kathy Baxendale, Nick Duffy and Phil Healey

Contents

Liquid gold?	2
Water sources	4
How much water do we need?	6
Water usage around the world	8
More people need more water	10
Drought and shortages	12
Running dry	14
Waste and pollution	16
Freshwater habitats	18
Water wars?	20
Global measures	22
How can we help save water?	24
Being water-efficient	26
How can technology help?	28
Remember – it's liquid gold!	30
Index	32

Liquid gold?

What is the most precious thing in your home? Is it your computer, the television, or the DVD player? There is something far more precious than these, because we cannot live without it. But we use it every day, and take it for granted.

It is the fresh clean water that comes out of our taps.

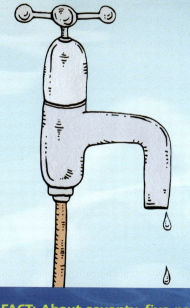

We need water for drinking, cooking and washing. We use it in our homes, in schools, in offices and factories.

FACT: You could live for two months without food, but for less than a week without water.

FACT: About seventy-five per cent of your brain is water!

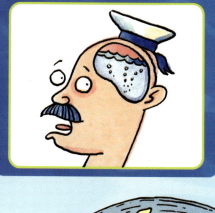

A lot of water is wasted, because people don't think about where it comes from, or where it goes when they flush it away. They imagine there is plenty of water because we live on a blue planet: seventy-five per cent of the Earth's surface is covered by water. But nearly all of that water is salty water in seas and oceans. Just three per cent of the Earth's water is freshwater, and most of that is locked up in the polar ice caps or deep inside the Earth. That leaves just over one per cent of the Earth's water for us to use!

trapped in ice caps and glaciers — usable water

oceans and seas

Water sources

The Earth has only so much freshwater. The water we use comes from rivers and lakes, underground sources or springs. In the developed world, it has to be pumped out then cleaned and treated and piped to our homes before we can drink it. When we flush it away, the water has to be purified. On its way to and from our homes, about thirty per cent of our water supply may be wasted because of leaking pipes.

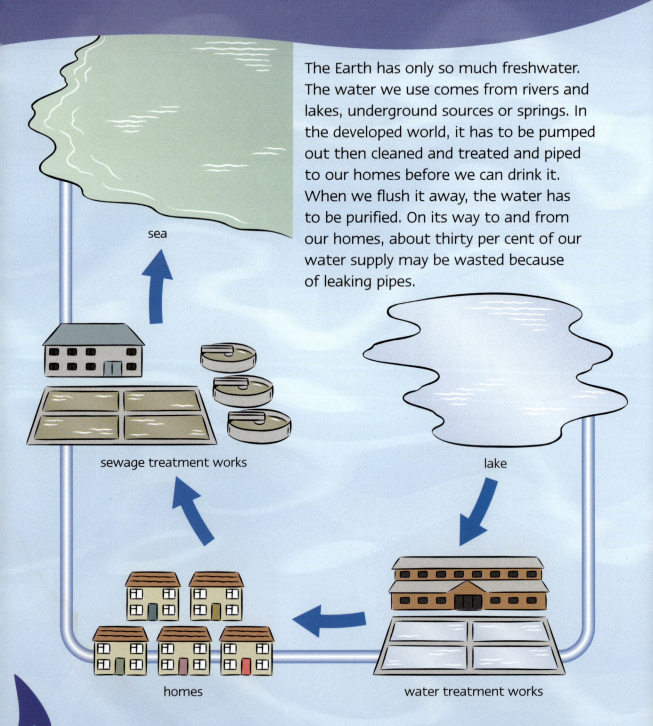

FOCUS: Recycled water

The freshwater on Earth is used over and over again in the water cycle. The sun heats water in rivers, lakes and oceans and turns some of it into water vapour. As air rises it cools and forms clouds. The water vapour turns back into droplets then falls as rain, hail or snow. Some of it runs into lakes, rivers and streams. We call this surface water. The rest soaks into the ground as groundwater.

FACT: It takes a water company up to forty-five minutes to produce one glass of water for us to drink!

How much water do we need?

We need about two to three litres of water a day to drink (although few of us drink even this much), and twenty litres for washing and cooking. But we don't just use water to drink or to wash ourselves.

FACT: For a city with a million people, 500,000,000 litres of water are needed every day.

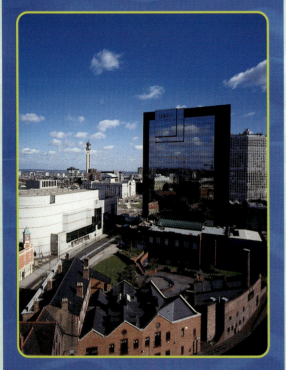

The city of Birmingham has a population of approximately one million people.

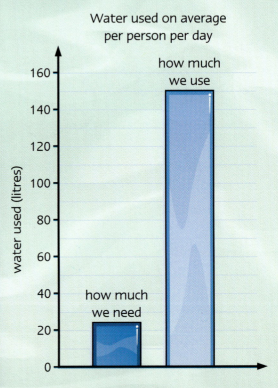

Water used on average per person per day

We use up to fifty litres of water every time we take a shower, or 160 litres if we take a bath. Every time we flush the toilet, we use ten litres of water. A dishwasher uses about eighty litres of water – twice as much as washing the same amount of dishes by hand; and a washing machine uses around 70 litres of water to clean our clothes. If we turn on the garden sprinkler to keep our lawn green, it uses up to 1100 litres every hour!

We also use water to make food and for our other daily needs.

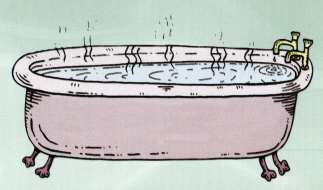

Having a bath uses up to 160 litres of water.

A five minute shower uses 50 litres of water.

A dishwasher uses 80 litres of water while washing dishes by hand takes half that amount.

A washing machine uses 70 litres of water per load.

FACT: It takes 5320 litres of water to produce a meal of a quarter pound hamburger, chips and a soft drink. This water is needed for the beef cattle to drink as well as for irrigating the crops that feed them. It is also used to water the potato crops to make the chips. Finally it is used for processing – such as cleaning the potatoes and producing the soft drink.

Water usage around the world

We are using more and more water every year around the world. The amount has increased because we are using more and more water each year for farming, for industry and for our homes. The water we use is doubling every twenty years.

About sixty-five per cent of all the water we use worldwide goes to **irrigate** crops for farming. We use lots of water to irrigate grain crops which we grow to feed cattle to produce beef. Twenty-four per cent of all our water is used for industry, to make things we use like cars and petrol. About seven per cent is used in our homes, and the rest – about four per cent – is wasted.

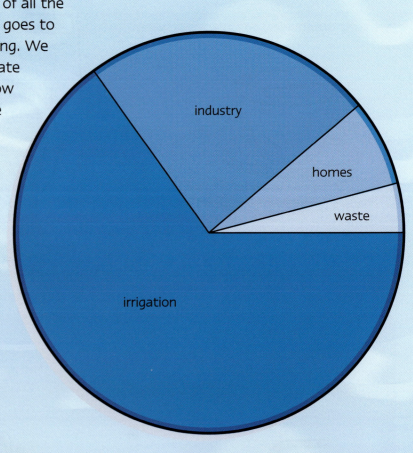

This chart shows the breakdown of water usage in the world.

GLOSSARY

irrigate provide water for plants

Experts estimate that the amount of water we use for industry and agriculture will double between 2005 and 2025. This is because the world population is growing fast, so there will be more of us needing goods and food.

FACTS
- It takes 1000 tons of water to produce just one ton of grain.
- It takes 100 litres of water to produce one kilogram of steel, much of which is used in the cooling process.

Steel is used to make many things

Steel ropes were used to make the second Severn Bridge.

Steel is used to make everyday items such as pots and pans.

Steel is used to make many kinds of boats, including large passenger ferries.

Steel is used to make cars; the steel from old cars can be recycled to make new cars.

More people need more water

The world needs more water because every year there are more of us. In the year 2000, there were six billion people on Earth. It is estimated that there will be eleven billion people by 2050. We all need water to live. But as the population grows, there is less water available for each of us. The amount of water available for each person has already fallen by one third since 1970.

As the population grows, there is less water available for each of us.

In 2050 the population of the Earth could be over 11 billion.

Today   2050

About eighty countries around the world already suffer from drought and water shortages. Countries where there is little rainfall and where the population is growing fast face the worst problems.

Experts believe that by 2025, two thirds of the world's population could live in countries facing water shortages. That means that two in every three people may not have enough water.

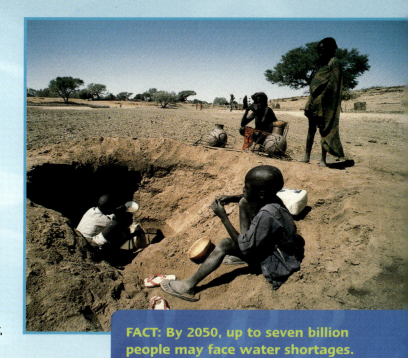

FACT: By 2050, up to seven billion people may face water shortages.

Worldwide potential water shortage, 2050

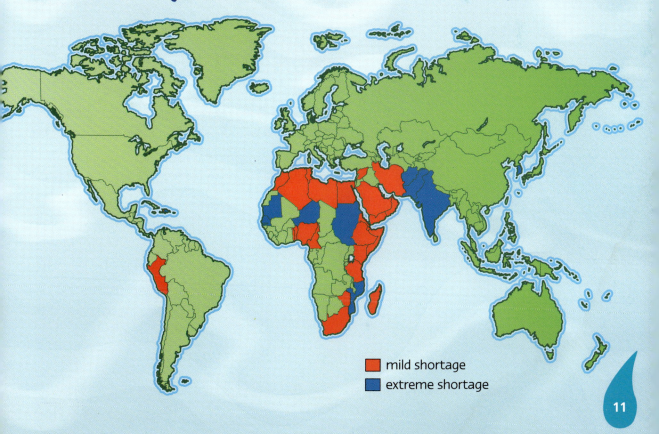

mild shortage
extreme shortage

Drought and shortages

Some areas have more water available than others. A lot of rain falls in areas like the Amazon and Congo river basins, where few people live. But in dry developing countries, where forty per cent of the world's population live, there can be long periods of drought.

During a drought, the earth can become so dry that it forms cracks.

The Amazon rain forest

FACTS

- In India, some households spend a quarter of their **income** on water.
- In some parts of Mexico, fresh water is so scarce that babies and children are given cola to drink instead.
- 1.1 billion people in the world do not have access to a fixed water supply.

GLOSSARY

income money earned

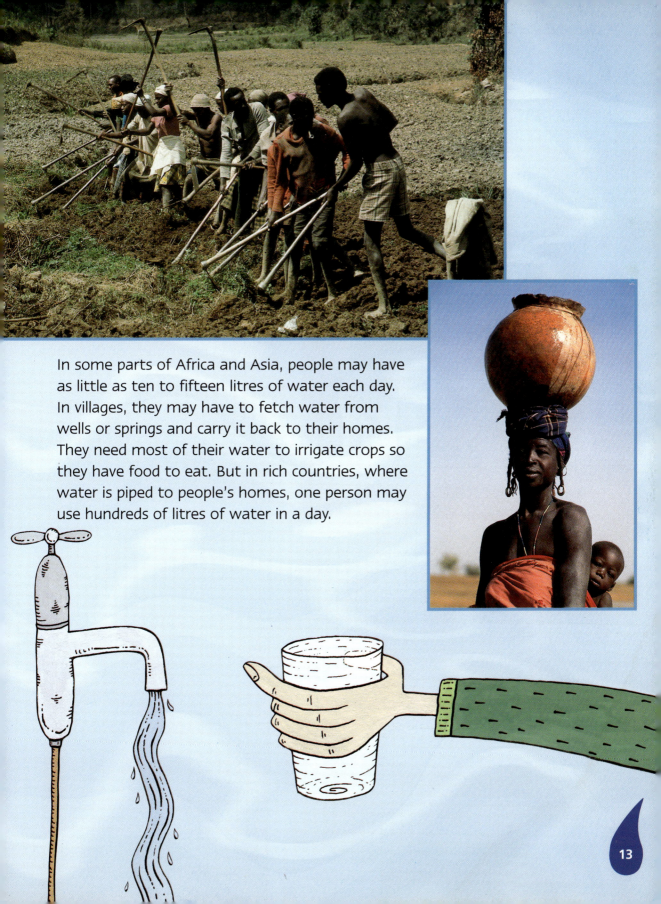

In some parts of Africa and Asia, people may have as little as ten to fifteen litres of water each day. In villages, they may have to fetch water from wells or springs and carry it back to their homes. They need most of their water to irrigate crops so they have food to eat. But in rich countries, where water is piped to people's homes, one person may use hundreds of litres of water in a day.

Running dry

Dams are built to block a river's flow so that water can be stored for us to use.

As we use more and more water, **reservoirs** are shrinking. In some countries we are pumping water out from underground reservoirs faster than it can be replaced by rainfall. This means that levels of groundwater are falling in many parts of the world.

A dried up river bed of the River Nile

We are also taking too much water from rivers. Dams and diversions of river water to irrigate farm land or supply industry mean that even great rivers like the Nile in Egypt, the Ganges in India and the Colorado in the United States sometimes run dry before they reach the sea.

GLOSSARY

reservoir large natural or man-made lake used for water supplies

As the ice caps melt, sea levels will rise and overflow on to the land. The sea will mix with freshwater in lakes and rivers, making them unusable.

Global warming may also reduce the amount of freshwater available to us. Warmer temperatures make water evaporate faster and salty water will invade the land because of rising sea levels.

We must reduce the amount of water we are using, or soon we will need more water than we have available to us.

FACT: Already, 300 cities in China do not have enough water for all the people.

Waste and pollution

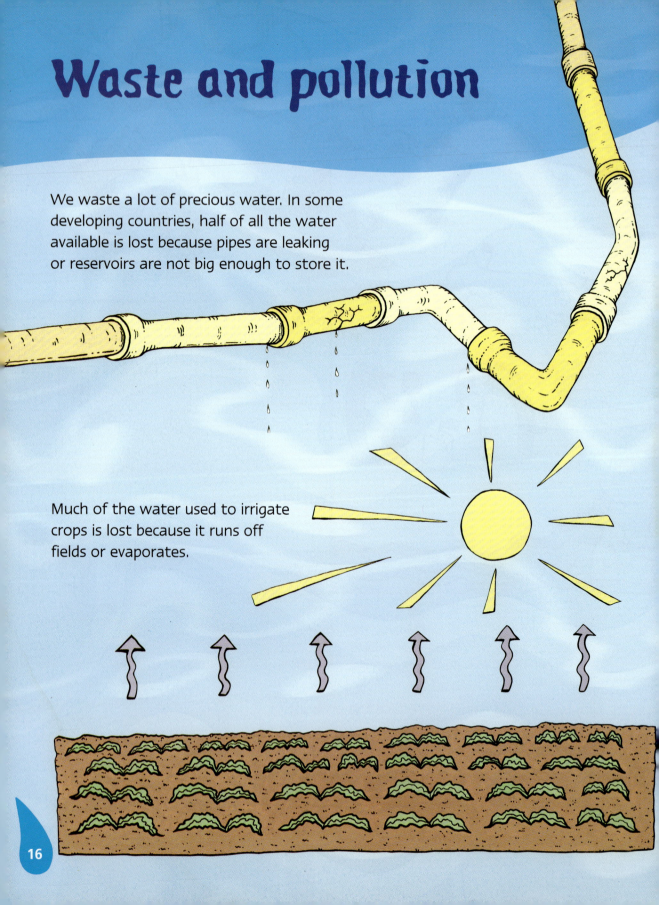

We waste a lot of precious water. In some developing countries, half of all the water available is lost because pipes are leaking or reservoirs are not big enough to store it.

Much of the water used to irrigate crops is lost because it runs off fields or evaporates.

We also waste water by polluting it. We pollute water with chemicals and pesticides used for farming, with industrial waste from factories and mines, and with untreated sewage. Pollution sometimes poisons the water in rivers, springs and wells.

FACT: A dripping tap can waste up to thirty litres of water a day.

Freshwater habitats

wetlands

The world's wetlands are vital for our supply of freshwater. They act like giant sponges, absorbing rainfall then slowly releasing it as freshwater. They help purify our water, and control flooding.

Wetlands occur when water meets land, and then they mix.

Wetlands are important environments for people, animals and plants. Most inland cities are built near a river or lake. People use the water for their homes, for farming, transport, power, and dumping waste. Wetlands are also important wildlife habitats for fish, birds and plants. Nearly half of the world's species of fish and many animal species live in freshwater habitats.

In the last 100 years, we have destroyed around half of the world's wetlands. We are destroying them by building dams, by draining land for farming and development, and by pollution and over fishing. Destroying wetlands means we are losing more of our precious freshwater supplies.

FACT: Wetlands cover just one per cent of the Earth's surface.

By destroying wetlands, we are endangering the lives of animals such as the Blue Duck and the Red Breasted Goose.

FACT: Less than ten per cent of all wetlands are protected by conservation measures.

The Wildfowl and Wetlands Trust (WWT) has set up centres all over the country to protect our wetlands and their wildlife.

Water wars?

As there are more and more of us, and less water to go round, people will start competing for the water they need. In the twenty-first century, water will be dangerously short in areas like Saudi Arabia, Central Asia and south-western parts of the USA. Water shortages could lead to **conflict** and war.

Some people believe that the wars of this century will be over water.

In Europe, there have been problems between Hungary and Slovakia over the damming of the River Danube.

A war could break out between Egypt and Ethiopia over Nile river water.

In Africa, Namibia and Botswana came into conflict over Namibia's plans to divert water from the Okavango river.

In many parts of the world, such as areas around Beijing in China and New Delhi in India, farmers increasingly have to compete with growing city populations for their water needs.

GLOSSARY

conflict fight or struggle

Global measures

We must find ways to stop waste and save water.

We use almost two thirds of all our water for farming. We could reduce the amount we use for irrigation by growing more cereal crops to feed people, rather than growing grain to feed beef cattle.

FACTS:
- **It takes 800 litres of water to produce one kilogram of wheat.**
- **It takes 30,000 litres of water to produce one kilogram of beef.**

We must also find more efficient ways of watering crops. The most efficient way is drip irrigation. A drip feed sends water to the roots of the plants where it is needed. Computers can control the amount so plants get just the water they need. We can also try to harvest and store more rainwater.

FACT: Drip irrigation is used for less than one per cent of the world's irrigated crops.

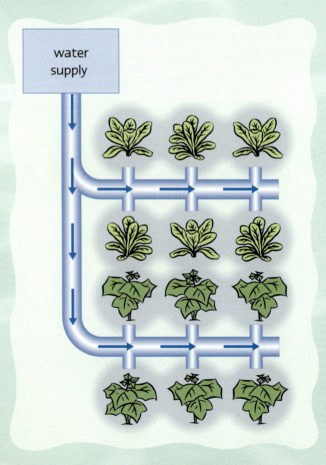

Drip irrigation

We must also use water for industry more efficiently. Most of the water used in manufacturing is to cool machinery and materials. This water could be recycled. We could clean waste water from industry and use it for irrigation.

waste water from industry

recycle and use in farming

We must also prevent and control water pollution, and make polluters pay to clean up their waste. Technology can help us clean and recycle water.

In future, we may need to make more freshwater by desalination. This means treating seawater to remove the salt.

23

How can we help save water?

We must all help to save water so there is enough to go round in the future. Every day, we each use about 150 litres of water in our homes and gardens.

We use much more water than we used to because of all the modern appliances in our homes, like flush toilets, washing machines, dishwashers and power showers.

A third of all that water goes down the toilet! Some modern toilets have low flush systems that use no more than six litres each time. You can help reduce wastage by putting a brick in the cistern so less water is used for each flush.

Take a shower rather than a bath – it uses less than half the water. But remember that a power shower will use more than a bath in less than five minutes.

Only use the washing machine and the dishwasher when they have a full load. We can also choose to buy water-efficient machines. Some washing machines use only thirty-six litres of water to wash a load, while others use over seventy litres! Washing clothes or dishes by hand saves even more water.

Being water-efficient

How can you help?

We all need to think of ways we can save water every day. Don't leave the tap running while you are cleaning your teeth – it can waste up to nineteen litres of water a day.

When it is hot and dry, we can use as much as half of all our household water in the garden. Sprinklers waste a lot of water just to keep lawns green. They can use 1100 litres every hour – as much water as a family of four uses in two days! Use a watering-can rather than a hose to water plants and best of all, water them using wastewater from washing or washing up.

You can also use rain butts to store rainwater for the garden.

Using a hose to wash the car also wastes lots of water – a hose can use as much as thirty-three buckets of water!

Check that there are no leaks from taps or pipes. If you see a leaking tap, report it so it can be mended.

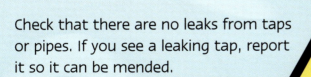

'Check your taps!'

How can technology help?

We need to find new kinds of technology to help us save and recycle more water. In Tokyo and other cities in Japan, some houses now have "grey water" recycling systems installed. Grey water is the water that we have used in our showers, baths and washbasins. These systems recycle the water and use it for flushing the toilet. They can save about a third of all the water we use daily.

Grey water can be used for watering plants, flushing the toilet and washing the car.

Technology may also help us make new freshwater. Desalination plants treat seawater to remove the salt so we can use it as freshwater.

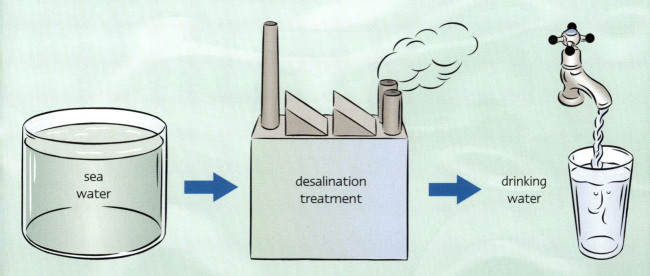

As there is so much water in the oceans, desalination is a good way of making new freshwater, although it is very expensive.

Remember – it's Liquid Gold

Water is so precious it is like liquid gold. There is less and less water for each person every year, so we must learn to stop wasting water, and to save the water we have and manage it well.

We have less water each year because:

- the world population is growing fast every year – every time the population doubles, the amount of water available for each person halves
- we are polluting and wasting water
- we are damaging freshwater habitats which help supply freshwater.

If we go on using more and more water, it will become dangerously scarce in some parts of the world. This could lead to competition and even wars over water.

Because it is "on tap", we often take water for granted. We think about it only when there is a drought, and water has to be rationed. But we must remember every day how precious water is, and treat it like liquid gold!

A Water Charter

- **Water belongs to the Earth and all its species** ✓
- **Water must be conserved for all time** ✓
- **Polluted water must be cleaned and re-used** ✓
- **Water should be left for local use wherever possible** ✓
- **Having enough fresh water is a basic human right** ✓

Index

Africa 11, 12, 13, 21
Asia 11, 13, 20, 21

baths 6, 7, 25
birdlife 19

cars 8, 9, 27
conflict and war 20–21
crops irrigation 8, 13, 16, 22

damaged habitats 30
dams 14, 15, 19, 21
demand 6–9, 13, 22
desalination 23, 29
dishwashers 6, 7, 24, 25
drought 11–13, 14

garden watering 6, 26
global warming 15
"grey water" 28

hoses 26, 27

ice caps 3, 15
industrial wastewater 8, 9, 23
irrigation 13, 14, 16, 22

leaks 2, 4, 16, 17, 27

pollution 17, 23, 30, 31
population growth 6, 9, 10–11, 30

rain 5, 12, 27
rainforest 12
recycling water 5, 23, 28–29
reservoirs 14, 16
rivers 5, 12, 14, 17, 19, 21

saving water 22–29
sewage treatment 4, 17
shortages of water 11–13, 14, 20
showers 6, 7, 24, 25
sources of water 4–5, 18–19
steel production 9
surface water 3, 5

taps 2, 13, 16, 17, 26, 27
technology 23, 28–29
toilets 6, 24, 28
treatment of water 4, 5

uses of water 3, 6–9

war 20–21
washing machines 6, 7, 24, 25
wastewater 8, 9, 23
wasting water 16–17, 30
water charter 31
water cycle 5
wetlands 18–19